Malcolm MacEuen

A Mosaic from Italy

And Other Poems

Malcolm MacEuen

A Mosaic from Italy
And Other Poems

ISBN/EAN: 9783744665643

Printed in Europe, USA, Canada, Australia, Japan

Cover: Foto ©Thomas Meinert / pixelio.de

More available books at **www.hansebooks.com**

A MOSAIC FROM ITALY,

And Other Poems.

BY

MALCOLM MACEUEN.

PHILADELPHIA:

MASON & CO.

No. 907 CHESTNUT STREET.

1867.

CAXTON PRESS OF
SHERMAN & CO., PHILADELPHIA.

CONTENTS.

TRANSLATIONS:

THESE POEMS

ARE DEDICATED TO THOSE WHOSE

AFFECTION

.

SUGGESTED AND ENCOURAGED

THEM.

1*

INVOCATION.

A TRAIL of robes! A flash of plumes!
A fragrance shed from rich perfumes!
    The Goddess sweeps along!
On her brow a star of fire;
In her hand a golden lyre:
The vaulting cadence flashes higher,
    And quivers into song!

Welcome, Goddess! Come and sing!
Make the heavenly changes ring!
    I have need to-night
Rest a while in this poor room:
I would fain forget my doom.
Oh, dissipate the deadening gloom
    With thy celestial light!

Round thy head is glory rolled;
The sandals on thy feet are gold:
     Oh, thou art fair to see!
Inmate of a holier sphere,
I marvel much to find thee here,
Translating thus to mortal ear
     Immortal harmony!

A MOSAIC FROM ITALY.

———————

DOWN through the snowy passes of the Alps,
Two lovers came upon the plains of Lombardy;
Leaving behind monastic St. Bernard,
High up the pass beside the gloomy lake:
—Stern outpost of heroic charity
Alone among the charging avalanches.—
Far fairer scenes awaited their approach
Where genial Italy unlocked her arms,
And spread her treasures to their dazzled sight.
A wondrous land! Where glory often clings
Brighter around some capitalless shaft,
Than flashes in crown diamonds. On they rode;
It seemed to them the very beggar boy
With tawny skin and laughing eye, that ran

9

Half clad beside the carriage, as they passed,
And hailed *la signorina,* while she dropped
A few *baiocche* in his outstretched palm,
Appeared less servile in his mendicancy,
Than beggars they had seen in other lands.
That *contadina* with her nursing child,
Sitting beside the fountain, 'neath the vines,
Might have been sketched by Raphael; for the past
Seemed to have sprung up round them in a moment.
The recollection of such golden days
Was sweetly treasured in their hearts; but when,
After long years had passed, one of the twain
Returned—alas! alone—to see these scenes,
His manhood could not curb the starting tear
Forced ever by remembrance, so he turned
His mournful steps to visit other lands
Which *she* had not made sacred by her presence.
They saw the great cathedral at Milan,
—Petrified poetry, rising into air,
For even the unlettered to peruse :—
And Pisa's tower inclined its archéd rings
As if to nod approval of their loves.
Lorenzo's Florence welcomed their approach,

When the moon rested on Fiesole,
With the eternal galleries where Art
Wrestles with Nature and half conquers her.
They thought they could have dwelt forever there
If they but dwelt together. By the Arno,
In the Cascini, and through princely halls
Stored with majestic relics of the past,
They wandered; hand in hand at night,
But always heart to heart. Then on to Rome
Southward they sped. Ere long the lofty dome,
—"To which Diana's marvel was a cell,"—
Rose on their sight, and seemed to bar the way
With vast magnificence. Th' Eternal City
Surrounded them again with splendid awe,
More splendid 'mid her ruins. They heard enchanted
That Roman accent of the Tuscan tongue,
Of which the poets boast. Then were they glad
They did not stay at Florence. At the portal
Of great St. Peter's church they paused awhile,
Between the circling colonnades there, by the foun-
        tains,
And the tall obelisk, ashamed to enter;
The structure seemed so vast, and they so small.

At last they crept like bees into a hive,
And held their breath and speech; they could but see,
And hardly see enough.   The heaving forms
That Michael Angelo has left behind,
Were there to startle them with all their grandeur,
And Raphael's living pictures bade them worship:
On every side dead centuries, to this,
Bequeathed their claims to immortality.
It was beyond description.   In the Vatican,
Bewildered through the galleries they went,
And saw the wounded Dacian die for them
As he has died for millions.   Endless death!
Then from a common page, with mutual eyes,
They read, intoning deftly worded lines,
About that other gladiator niched
By Byron in the Vatican of Fame.
Laocöon reared for them his struggling form
Between the wreathing serpents; his two sons
Strangled beside him.   Thus are apt to slay
Hereditary evils sire and child alike.
They stood enraptured by Medici's Venus
—Embodiment of every line of grace.—
O peerless Aphrodité!   In all lands

Thy charms are known, and still thy daughters live;
Mortals are made to feel their power too,
And bow the knee before resistless beauty.
But who can tell of Rome? Where every Art,
After maturing for a thousand years,
Bursts full upon the world with luscious ripeness.
Southward the lovers travelled. Soon they saw
A lovely bay—felucca-speckled azure—
With Naples basking on the curvéd shore
That bends to old Vesuvius in full view.
The mountain sloped up to a point, where puffed
A jet of smoke, shaped like a water-spout,
That broad'ning rose up to a turquoise sky
And disappeared at last in the still air.
The pleasant sea extended leagues around
To mirror-gleaming islands. On the hills,
Green vines came down to mingle with white houses,
While every thing breathed peaceful loveliness.
With the approach of evening all this changed.
The dying sun fell like a gladiator
Upon his golden shield, all gules, and left
Earth, sky, and water, purple with his gore.
Vede Napoli e poi mori, seemed

Emblazed and flashing everywhere, until
The eye grew tired of admiration. All that night
They dreamed of burning mountains and bright seas;
And lingered long in Naples. Then they turned
Northward again, to visit peerless Venice.
They found the sea-queen, sitting in her glory
Among the islands, while a crescent moon
Dipped on her brow as though she were Diana
Resting beside the ocean. Here they tarried
Until the crescent swelled to a full orb,
That flooded the piazza and canals
With trembling light. Sometimes they shot along,
Cutting the gloomy shadows of the bridges
With their swift gondola; and once they took
A larger bark, to greet the classic islands
Far down the gulf. Returning from this trip,
They landed at a village of the coast,
And climbed the rocks to see a little chapel
Perched on the heights above. A simple building
It proved to be; devoid of ornament,
Save votive offerings grouped round the altar;
And a large crucifix rudely carved in wood;
Such as are often seen in Italy

Erected by the roadside.   They observed
That in the pale Christ's side a crimson stain
Appeared, and this was covered by a glass,
So as to guard it from all injury.
Wondering what this could mean, they looked around
For some one to explain it.   A peasant woman,
Just risen from her knees beside the altar,
Was passing out: she stopped surprised when ques-
      tioned.
"You must be strangers here indeed," she said,
"Not to have heard about the miracle
That makes our chapel known through all the
      country;
And many pilgrims come from other lands
To worship at this shrine.   That cross you see
Stood once uncovered by the road; the little church
Has been built over it.   This is the story:—
Hundreds of years ago, when this whole region
Was full of robbers, and bloodthirsty pirates
That came up from the sea, a brace of cut-throats
Sat down one afternoon beneath the cross
To play at dice, and pass the time away.
One of the villains lost each time he threw,

Until at last he rose in wrath, and cursed
The Christ upon the cross. He swore that if
He lost another round, he'd take a stone
And hurl it at the crucifix. They sat,
And played again, and still again he lost.
Then, with a great oath, springing up, he picked
A stone from off the road, and struck the Christ
Just in the side there, where you see that stain.
But do not think the crime was unavenged.
A stream of blood poured from the wounded side
—As when the Roman soldier fixed his spear—
And reddened all the ground. The opening earth
Swallowed up quick the sacrilegious pair,
With shrieks and flame of fire. You must believe
This miracle, for there you see the blood,
And here we stand upon the very spot
Where this was done. So has our chapel honor,
And many wondrous cures are still performed
On those who seek this shrine." With these words
She went her way, and left them pondering
On the strange legend, till advancing night
Stole on them unawares. The lady seemed
Silent and sad; her husband asked the cause,

Looking his question in her eyes. "Alas!"
She said, "how many of us now,
With more advantages than these poor men,
Do daily stone Christ in our hearts; and yet
We still live on, unpunished for our sin!"
He made no answer, but in silence took
Her little hand in his; and slowly thus
They wandered shoreward, lighted by the stars.

REMINISCENCE.

IT is a pleasant fancy, that invests
Inanimate things with life, attributing
The power to feel such sentiments as we
Ourselves have felt while gazing upon them:
For thus they seem to share our joy and pain.
Who ever wandered thro' an antique house,
Time-worn and shattered, like a broken heart,
Where only echoes live of loves that were,
But felt the strange, mysterious beckoning
Of shadowy hands stretched from a shadowy past,—
That called him from the active, busy Now,
Into the bosom of some bygone Then?
Why does it wound our sensibilities
To see old mansions rudely tumbled down,

18

And grand old chambers, that have long been silent,
Thrown open to the uproar of the street,
And clownish criticism of the mob;
But that we deem them proudly reticent,
Tapestried with the thoughts of other days,
And umbraged at these rough indignities?
Why do we hang upon a faded flower,
And treasure it, but that there seems to cling
Still to its withered petals power to bring
Some perfume from a still more faded past?
Lost loves and buried friendships! Ye are gone.
But still I fancy, in the vacant cells
Ye left within my heart, I hear again
Some echo of your former minstrelsy!
So let me hold you sacred for the joys
With which ye once have gilded parted hours.
(For love, though lost, is like a precious jewel:
We light a candle, and sweep diligently
To try if we can find it; for we know
That the lost jewel still must glitter somewhere.
And friendship may be buried quick, and stir
Uneasily within its sepulchre,
Though it may fail to burst the marble tomb.)

Still are there certain seasons consecrate
To hallowed mem'ries, such as make a calm
Amid the storm and bustle of our lives;
Like silent chapels in a busy street,
Forgotten in the turmoil of the day,
But sought with rev'rent, contemplative steps
When vesper hymns arise to meet the stars.

Thus I sit here alone.   The midnight bell
Bids yesterday good-by, and summons up
—As in past years at such memorial time—
A phantom-like procession of pale thoughts,
On which I gaze and ponder, till they grow
So life-like I could almost rise and grasp them.
I see again the lustre of an eye
That once I thought were always bright for me;
And hear again the music of a voice
That once I thought for me were never silent;
And feel again the pressure of a hand
That once I thought would always welcome me.
So the still hours glide on the stream of night,
How fast or slow I reck not, for I sit,
Bewildered by these visions of the heart,

Holding old relics in my drooping hands,
Until the banners of ghost-scaring morn
Advance their oriental gold and purple.
Then slowly,—slowly,—as my eyelids fall,
The pinion-spreading phantoms soar away,
Shaking from out their wings some plumes of song,
That flutter down and lull to dreamy sleep.

Again! again! We clasp our hands together,
    O days of long ago!
And hail the gleaming of a sunset river
    Where happy waters flow!

The day-god stoops among the murmuring rushes,
    With glory multifold;
Kissing the earth, like Danäe, all blushes,
    Beneath a shower of gold!

Again! again! How could ye leave me ever?
    To be remembered so!
We drained no Lethean goblet from that river,
    O days of long ago!

A BIRTHDAY WAIF.

THE well-poised axle of the car of Time
   Rolls down the length'ning avenue of years,
Scythe-armed and silent. Juggernaut sublime!
Crushing an empire now; now drying woman's tears.
     Human Art with Nature strives
     To chronicle our changing lives:—
     Reveillée from fortress wall,—
     Sunset gun and bugle call,—
     Pond'rous stroke in minster spire,—
     Tinkle o'er the parlor fire,—
     Faithful shadow creeping round
     The gnomon in yon pleasure-ground,—
     Attest how man exerts his skill
     To track the foe he cannot kill.

Nature on a mightier scale
Reiterates her oft-told tale:—
Rising blast and falling leaf,—
Empty field and garnered sheaf,—
Flight of birds to balmier homes,—
Who runs could read that Autumn comes.

When the Winter King appears,
With all his glittering spears,
And a thousand snowy banners in his train,
He finds the giant oaks,
Having doffed their leafy cloaks,
Stand prepared to dispute his right to reign.

They toss their arms on high,
Athwart the murky sky,
And howl grim defiance from afar;
Then he charges o'er the plain,
And we seem to see again
The Titans and the Gods waging war.

But I do not need the sight
Of this elemental fight

To remind me that Winter comes at last;
   For pleasant thoughts arise,
   Unsubdued by leaden skies,
Encouraged by the moaning of the blast.

   Be my carrier-pigeon, gale!
   Fly over hill and dale,
Till you come to stately Alverthorpe's fair seat;
   Take these leaves upon your wings,
   Among other worthless things,
And drop them at my cousin's little feet!

   Haste, haste! You must not stay!
   Bear my love to her to-day,
And whisper gentle greetings in her ear;
   May old Tempus, in his flight,
   Prove powerless to blight
The happiness in store for many a year!

MAJOR CHARLIE,

Killed in battle, March, 1865.

THY golden leaflet withers and dies
   While yet it is sparkling with dew;
May thy star be won in the glorious skies,
   Soldier-brother so gallant and true!

Though each falling leaf will recall to my sight
   Thy fate in these horrible wars,
I'll dry my eyes when each darksome night
   Becomes lighted with glittering stars.

In the land of the blest, where all spirits are free
   From distinction of gray or of blue,
Christ grant we may meet at the great reveillée,
   Soldier-brother so gallant and true!

It may not be mine to lay wreaths on thy hearse,
As thou goest embalmed in thy fame.
Let me gather at least my poor chaplet of verse
And consecrate it to thy name.

CHRISTMAS POEMS.

CHRISTMAS EVE.

THE church-bells, swung in olden times,
Peal out again in splendid chimes;
Spreading, like surges, sound on sound,
Till every hamlet steeple round
    Acknowledges the call.
With midnight mass cathedrals glow;
The stars salute the earth below;
        On distant moor,
        The maiden poor
Hangs holly on the wall.

'Tis Christmas Eve! Who could be sad?
All earth, at such a time, is glad!
Where is the heart, cuirassed in steel,
On Christmas Eve that cannot feel

3*

Some nobler pulse within?
If piercing blow the winter wind,
Let it but waft our guilt behind;
    We feel more clear
    From care and fear,
And further from each sin.

Cousin! I frankly say to you
There is one thing I cannot do:
I cannot thank, as it deserves,
Kindness like yours, that never swerves,
  Although abused and tried.
But I, at least, can wish you here
Many and many and many a year
    Of every joy,
    Without alloy,
And "Merry Christmas-tide."

CHRISTMAS EVE.

TO-NIGHT, above the silent rill,
And frosty trees, and distant hill,
There glimmers in the sky a star
That shone, oh, long ago! afar,
And taught some shepherds where to seek,
The while they heard the angels speak
Celestial words that echo still:—
"Peace upon earth; to men good will."

What though the woods, invoked to share
Our joy, no richer tribute bear
Than holly-leaves and evergreen?
Our hearts have nobler gifts, I ween.
For mortals now returning see
The Eve of Christ's Nativity.

Though voiceless be the ice-bound rill,
The waves of thought have music still.
Oh that my tiny pebble, thrown
Into the stream of Song alone,
May make the widening circles glance
Till at thy feet the wavelets dance!
Let every undulation be
A Christmas carol sung to thee.

What though the trees with branches bare
Trellis the frosty Christmas air?
Still Recollection flaunts on high
Her gorgeous banner 'gainst the sky;
And still, above the gathering storm,
Affection's heart throbs loud and warm.
Dear cousin! Once again, receive
My thanks and love, on Christmas Eve.

GASPS the dying poet: "Give me a great thought,
　To cheer me ere my drooping spirit part."
Cries the pallid lover: "Give me a great hope,
　To fill the gloomy void within my heart."
Sobs the blushing maiden: "Give me a great love,
　Such as the angels waft from heaven to earth."
Pants the falling soldier: "Give me a great fame,
　To blaze the story of my martial worth."
Ye human aspirations, soaring high!
How many of you but shall fall and die
Like shaft-struck eagles? Therefore let my task,
If pleasure can be task, O lady, be to ask
Something that may be granted. For I know your
　　heart
Pours out a stream of bounty unto all. Now, do
　　not start.
I crave this Christmas Eve a gift. Oh, may there be
A little place kept in your heart for even me!

C　　　　　　　　　　　　　　　　　　　33

THE CHRISTMAS DRUM.

I HAVE read an odd legend of other climes,
How invisible bells ring the Christmas chimes,
How a ghostly bugle at midnight calls
Through the tapestried reaches of echoing halls,
And phantom armies at midnight come
Prompt at the tap of a phantom drum.

If this mute little drum had but power to resound,
And give form to the wishes now thronging around,
An army of blessings should spring into ranks,
Whole legions of love, and a squadron of thanks,
While aloft in the banner this motto should shine:—
"Merry Christmas, fair Lady, to thee and to thine."

34

THE FLOWER OF CHILLON.

A DOWN a dismal winding stair,
    That led to depths below,
A lady, blooming, young, and fair,
From distant lands a pilgrim there,
With pensive brow and stately air,
    Swept mournfully and slow.

No sunbeam on that castle wall
    Was brighter than her smile;
She lighted up the echoing hall,
That scarce repeated her footfall,
And Chillon's far-famed castle tall
    Might well be glad the while.

35

O mighty Chillon, in thy pride
  Bedecked with legends gray!
O lovely Leman, by whose side
The castle rises like a bride,
Mirror-reflected in thy tide!—
  I envy thee that day!

I envy thee the mem'ries hoar
  That cling around each stone;
And when the hand shall be no more
That pens these lines, there still shall pour
A stream of pilgrims through thy door,
  To worship at thy throne.

Thy fame is deathless, castle gray!
  Embalmed by Albion's bard,—
For sure immortal is his lay:
Can Byron's verses e'er decay?
Or can those fetters rust away
  That clanked on Bonnivard?

No! deathless are those notes of wrong,
  Struck by the master hand:

And while we listen to his song,
Forms that from buried ages throng,
Roused by his incantation strong,
    Living before us stand.

Onward the graceful lady swept,
    Filled with these thoughts sublime:
Through frowning arch, and sullen crypt,
By "loophole barred, where captives wept,"
And men at arms stern vigil kept,
    Back in the far old time.

But who can measure woman's heart,
    Or gauge its wondrous power?
Through her sweet spirit came a dart
Of vivid memory.   Far apart
From her, and all these stores of art,
    She thought of one that hour,

And gathered from the pavement old
    A flower.   Strange sight to see!
It grew from out a crevice cold,
As shivering lamb on wintry wold,

4

Shut out perchance from dam and fold,
Stands bleating piteously.

The sun that rises on Chillon
Rolls westward for to set.
That treasured flower now gladdens one
Immured within a fortress lone,
Within whose frowning tiers of stone
Its fragrance lingers yet.

And oft, when midnight surges swell,
Or midnight cannon booms,
The prisoner, waking in his cell,
Smiles as he frames fit words to tell
How still, renewed by fairy spell,
The Flower of Chillon blooms.

VALENTINE.

WHEN Summer decks the woods with green
  And sets the fields a smiling,
My Mary cheers the glowing scene,
  Unhappiness beguiling.
When boist'rous Winter plays his part,
  Still comes my precious fairy
And kindles summer in my heart,—
  My darling little Mary!

Oh that I had the magic power
  To warble like a poet!
I could not love my Mary more,
  But I could better show it:

39

I'd soar exultant all day long,
    Like eagle from her eyrie,
At night I'd bring my sweetest song
    And sing it to my Mary.

I'd pluck the gleaming fruit that hung
    All in Hesperian gardens,
And fairest flowers that odors flung,
    In spite of dragon wardens;
And many a tale grotesque I'd tell,
    Of gnome, or elf, or peri,—
A tribute to my little belle,
    A Valentine for Mary.

SONNETS.

SONNET.

'TIS pleasant sometimes, down the oubliette
    Oblivion kindly opens in our past,
To drop our sorrows; hardships to forget,
    And exorcise the spectres that would cast
Their blight upon our future.   Turn we still
    From passing darkness to the coming day;
    From the dense murk of midnight, to the ray
Of hope that soon must light the eastern hill.
    But, while we quaff nepenthe for the woes
That else, accumulating with our years,
Had overborne our manhood, there are tears
    Of joy we would not dry,—that flow for those
Whose constant kindness never ceased to shine,
A storm-wrapped beacon; kindness such as thine!

43

SONNET.

MADAM, dear madam! Surely I might claim
   Relationship with you, I call to mind
Such acts of kindness; and one of your name,
   If little less than kin, was more than kind;
(So let me travesty an ancient phrase
   To suit my grateful purpose.) Thus I try
To thank you, in these insufficient lays,
   For many an act of gentlest sympathy.
A year ago to-day, the gates that pent
   My freedom, held in ward by arméd men,
Flared open, and the beck'ning landscape sent
   A throb of gladness through my pulses then.
But all my fetters dropped not. Tighter grew
Affection's chain, that stretched 'twixt me and you!

THE Past and Present! How the pictures glow!
　　Like the old Danish portraits i' the play.
　But as stars vanish at the break of day,
　So fades the Present as the Past gains sway.
A name, a date, a face, the winds that blow
Odors of well-known flowers from well-known fields,—
Are all sufficient.　Then the Present yields
Her precedence: the active power she wields
Drops on the shoulders of the rising Past,
Till last becomes the first, the first the last.
To-day comes fraught with feeling; like a tune
　One learned in childhood, heard perchance again,
　After much tossing on a stormy main.
No wonder that it does: it is the Fourth of June!

EPIGRAM.

THE RELEASED PRISONER TO HIS MISTRESS.

THOUGH loosed from all prison, I still am
not free.

Come solve me this riddle, and tell me, what art
Thou hast used, my enslaver : I owe it to thee
That the chains from my hands are transferred
to my heart!

46

MY PRISON BY MOONLIGHT.

MY captive companions lie sleeping around,
   Forgetful a while of their sorrow and care;
The vault of our dungeon re-echoes no sound,
   Save the sentinel's tramp on the esplanade there.

The night is resplendent with moon and with stars,
   No cloud dims their lustre, no tempest is near;
As I creep to the casemate and gaze through the bars
   In wonder to witness such loveliness here.

The moon like a herald emblazons the sea,
   Bend argent traversing a 'scutcheon of blue;
And I know the same light that is shining on me
   Falls soft on the tower of fair Alverthorpe too.

The star-girdled empress, enthroned in the air,
    Touches fortress and tower with her bright-flashing
        blade,
And the earth seems to rise from the contact more
        fair,
    Like a warrior touched by a queen's accolade.

Such glory without, and such darkness within,
    What wonder the prisoner's heart turns away
From the sorrow that is, to the joy that has been,
    And still tinges with silver the cloud of to-day?

Though the bright sun of happiness hasten to set,
    —As a three-decker founders with banner and
        mast,—
The moonlight of memory lingers here yet,
    Blending hope for the future with love for the
        past;

Giving promise that morning will come once again,
    Bursting open the ponderous portals of night,
And reminding the captive that, loosed from his chain,
    He may bask in the sunshine of freedom and light.

That fair faces will greet his return with a smile,
   As he halts for repose on his wearisome track;
And kind voices will mingle in chorus the while,
   To welcome the prison-worn wanderer back.

.

5

AN ÆOLIAN SERENADE.

OH, whence comes that music that, stealing so
 gently,
Brings echoes of melodies long past away,
Like a choir chanting orisons grandiloquently,
 Or vesper-nuns sighing for moribund day?

Now low breathe the accents, as if pleasure-laden
 From gardens where young Love lies cradled in
  flowers,
Now high and prolonged, like the wail of a maiden
 Whose lover is dead in her desolate bowers.

A guitar at a scarce-opened window is lying,
 And the cool breeze of evening my serenade sings,

Weird æolian echoes through dream-land are flying,
    As the wing of the air-spirit brushes the strings.

Sure nowhere but in mediæval romance ye
    Could hope such fantastic conception to find;
Some wandering ghost of a troubadour's fancy
    This phantom-like roundelay taught to the wind.

Perchance cavaliers as a madrigal rang it
    Through balconied streets by the light of the stars,
Till palace-shrined beauty awoke, as they sang it
    To felicitous cadences on their guitars.

Knights, ladies, and troubadours sleep their last
        slumbers,
    For all soûvenir leaving this quaint melody;
Yet my fancy delights to imagine the numbers
    They loved, to be those the wind whispers to me.

THE RETARDED VERSES.

A PAIR of glittering slippers from the East,
From Nilus' bank,—where once the swarthy
belle,
Whose beauty made the Roman laurel bow
And do her homage, lived,—I bring to thee;
Not all uncertain—like that doubtful prince
Who followed Cinderella from the ball—
Whose foot may fit the bauble. Well I know
The graceful instep that will arch above
And decorate each decorated shoe.
Thy beauty needs no further garniture
To set it off, 'tis true; but, then, reflect
That these poor slippers, though they flash with gold,
Need still thy touch to ornament them more.

For their sake, then, if not for mine, accept them.
But sometimes, prythee, in thy happier mood,
When they are resting on thy little feet,
Think that thou seest th'unworthy donor there.

COMMENCEMENT.

ONCE a year, in the old town of Cambridge,
 There's a day when the Governor comes,
With aides-de-camp, sheriffs, and lancers,
 And clangor of trumpets and drums;

When the damsel who dwells in the city
 Comes out to embellish the scene;
And the maiden who lives in the cottage
 Trips college-ward over the green;

When students, from every direction,
 And white-headed men from afar,
Throng a building with wide-open portals,
 Like the temple of Janus in war.

54

And, begirt with a staff of professors,
   The President comes on that day,
Like an old academic field-marshal,
   To review the scholastic array.

Alma Mater, majestic and graceful,
   Enthroned 'mid her colleges gray,
Bestows a last kiss on her children,
   And sends them exultant away.

Though they tread the dim shores of the Ganges,
   Or explore the mysterious Nile;
Though the forests of "dark-rolling Danube"
   Their meandering footsteps beguile;

Though they fly on the wings of the morning
   To the uttermost isle of the sea;
Even there shall they bless Alma Mater,
   For there shall her influence be.

Ofttimes, when oppressed with affliction,
   Or disgusted with pleasure that palls,
They shall think with regret on the tranquil delights
   They resigned in those elm-shaded halls.

Two lustres have lapsed since we parted,
  Our mother, my classmates, and I:
Alas! Here I sit in the gloaming alone,
  And conjecture their fate with a sigh.

How many, I wonder, have "dreed their doom"?
  How many may still be alive?
Waes hael! Here I pledge ye, old comrades,
  Thou class of the year Fifty-five.

TRANSLATIONS.

SPANISH EPIGRAM.

A UNQUE en espejo se miran
Las mujeres con frequencia;
En mismo tiempo nunca ven
Que es de vidrio su belleza.

Ladies gaze in their mirrors as oft, I suspect,
  As though they considered it part of their duty;
But the darlings themselves never seem to reflect
  To what attribute glass owes its exquisite beauty.

59

THE SONG OF THE RHINE.

From the German.

COME fill the goblet! Round it ivy twine,
   And joyous drain it here!
Europe's broad empire boasts no other wine,
   Sirs-Revellers, its peer!

Not in the fields of laughter-loving France,
   Poland or Hungary:
St. Vitus may prefer those drinks, perchance;
   No wine grows there for me.

Our native country yields it from her treasure:
   How were it else so good?

60

Or how so calm and noble beyond measure
   With potent hardihood?

Even amid Germania's classic features
   Stand many mountains, still,
Just like their native reptiles, dirty creatures,
   Not worth the space they fill.

Thuringia's mountains, for example, offer
   A sort of stuff folks brew;
But that's not wine! On that no singing scoffer
   Rollicks till all is blue.

You'll search the ore-producing mountains vainly,
   If wine you would behold:
Cobalt and silver are their products mainly,
   Mixed with some spurious gold.

The Blocksberg's but a long-legged *cit*, with speeches
   Inflated and bombastic:
There Satan and his kindred crew of witches
   Cut up their shines fantastic.

But on the Rhine! The Rhine! Our vineyards
    cluster.
  All hail, transcendent Rhine!
Look, to the brink the leafy squadrons muster,
  And reel with glorious wine.

Then drain the beaker! Fill and drink again,
  Flushed with melodious glee!
We'll rouse the sick man from his couch of pain,
  To join our revelry.

LORELEI.

𝔉rom 𝔱𝔥𝔢 𝔊𝔢𝔯𝔪𝔞𝔫.

———

I CANNOT tell what it presages
   That I so sad should be;
But a legend of distant ages
   Still haunts my memory.
Cool breezes herald the coming night,
   The tranquil Rhine flows by,
The sparkling mountain-crest glows bright
   Where evening sunbeams die.

Enthroned in surpassing loveliness,
   A maiden is sitting there;
Golden ornaments flash in her dress,
   She is combing her golden hair,—

Combing her hair with a comb of gold,
  And singing a song, the while,
Whose mystic melody wondrous and bold
  Can mortal heart beguile.

The sailor is thrilled by her magical notes,
  And gazes bewildered on high,
Unheeding his shallop, that rapidly floats
  On the sunken rocks near by.
Sailor and shallop must perish amain
  Where the breakers are surging nigh;
For death and destruction lurk in the strain
  That is caroled by Lorelei.

ITALY.

From the German of Goethe.

KNOW'ST thou the land where the citron-trees
    grow,
In whose dark leafy groves golden oranges glow?
Where a soft air from heaven sweeps over the seas,
And the laurel and myrtle are fanned by the breeze?
Know'st thou it well? 'Tis there, oh! there,
That with thee, my darling, I fain would repair!

Know'st thou the palace with colonnade tall?
The rich trappings gleam through the glittering hall;
There statues of marble look kindly on me,
As if asking, "Poor child, what has happened to
    thee?"

65

Know'st thou it well? 'Tis there, oh! there,
That with thee, heart's treasure, my lot I would
    share!

Know'st thou the cloud-crested mountain so gray,
Where the sure-footed mule through the mist gropes
    its way?
The brood of the dragon lies hid in its caves,
ˌ And down the rent rock the wild cataract raves.
Know'st thou it well?   Thereby, thereby,
Our road leads, O father: away let us hie!

THE POWER OF SONG.

From the German.

———

IN those blest realms where Song her power re-
    veals,—
  It matters not for creed,—there fearless dwell:
Where song prevails, no lurking robber steals,
  For bad men's bosoms with no music swell.

Each mother consecrates with music mild
  To happy life her darling's earliest hours;
Through groves in May she leads the smiling child,
  And cradles him to sleep with songs of flowers.

In song the young man's passion bursts its bonds,
  And carols his unspeakable delight:

6*   67

How quick the loved one's conscious heart responds!—
  Music reveals what poet cannot write.

Old men sit at their doors with hoary head,
  And chant the wise men's songs in joyous tones;
No despot's minion fills their soul with dread,
  For song makes tyrants tremble on their thrones.

When round the grape-blood-brimming beaker flies,
  Shortening the hours amid the roses there,   -
If wisdom comes and tinctures all our joys,
  Then song completes a banquet gods might share.

The stripling leaves the master's hand and rings
  Loud song when rushing into spring-time fair;
While at the meadow-side the sister sings,
  Twining a wreath to deck her charmer's hair.

Men hang on beauty's smile-light sweet, and need
  No other charms to keep them at her feet;
But should the siren's soul-felt strain succeed,
  Oh, then indeed th'enchantment is complete.

With war-song fierce the hero grasps the brand
  When freedom's clarion high resounds for right;
Fenced in the steel-proof mail of duty's band,
  He dares to death the iron-hurtling fight.

Sweet Song! Thy soft, soul-guiding power soon
    brings
To end each evil that to toil belongs;
Under thy influence virtue's germ upsprings:—
  Oh, wretched, wretched land that has no songs!

THE END.

www.ingramcontent.com/pod-product-compliance
Lightning Source LLC
Chambersburg PA
CBHW030025030726
47499CB00008B/3129